FIRST
ARABIC HANDWRITING
WORKBOOK

by

Lily Sayegh

Published by:
International Book Centre
P.O. Box 295 • Troy, Michigan 48099

First Arabic Handwriting Workbook
l. Writing, Arabic. 1.Sayegh, Lily

PJ6321.F57 492'.7' 11   79-15238

ISBN 0-917062-03-5

Published by:
International Book Centre, Inc.
2007 Laurel Drive
P.O. Box 295
Troy, Michigan 48099 USA

To order our publications visit our website:
www.ibcbooks.com
E-mail: ibc@ibcbooks.com

The Arabic Alphabet
(read from right to left)

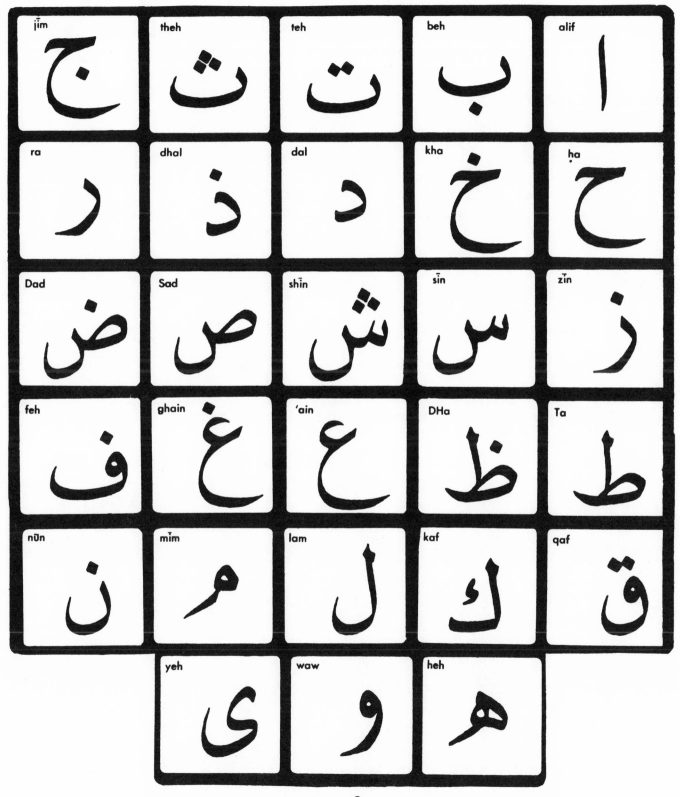

ALIF

PRONOUNCE AND PRACTICE WRITING.

أ ↓

The Shape of each letter changes depending on its position in a word.
Practice writing each form. **Arabic is written and read from right to left.**

END	MIDDLE	FIRST LETTER	STANDING ALONE
ا	أ	أ	أ

4

BEH

PRONOUNCE AND PRACTICE WRITING.

ب ب

END	MIDDLE	FIRST LETTER	STANDING ALONE
ـب	ـبـ	بـ	ب

TEH

PRONOUNCE AND PRACTICE WRITING.

ت

END	MIDDLE	FIRST LETTER	STANDING ALONE
ت or ة or ق	ﺘ	ﺗ	ت

ث

THEH

PRONOUNCE AND PRACTICE WRITING.

ثـ

END	MIDDLE	FIRST LETTER	STANDING ALONE
ـث	ـثـ	ثـ	ث

JĪM

PRONOUNCE AND PRACTICE WRITING.

جـ

END	MIDDLE	FIRST LETTER	STANDING ALONE
ـج	ـجـ	جـ	ج

HA

PRONOUNCE AND PRACTICE WRITING.

ح

END	MIDDLE	FIRST LETTER	STANDING ALONE
ح	ح	ح	ح

9

KHA

PRONOUNCE AND PRACTICE WRITING.

خٰ

END	MIDDLE	FIRST LETTER	STANDING ALONE
ـخ	ـخـ	خـ	خ

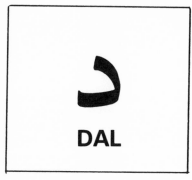

DAL

PRONOUNCE AND PRACTICE WRITING.

د↓

END	MIDDLE	FIRST LETTER	STANDING ALONE
ـد	ـد	د	د

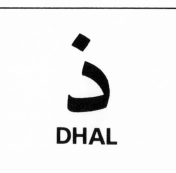

DHAL

PRONOUNCE AND PRACTICE WRITING.

ذ

END	MIDDLE	FIRST LETTER	STANDING ALONE
ـذ	ـذـ	ذ	ذ

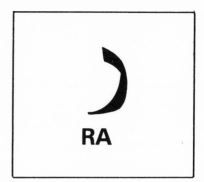

RA

PRONOUNCE AND PRACTICE WRITING.

END	MIDDLE	FIRST LETTER	STANDING ALONE
ر	ر	ر	ر

13

ZĪN

PRONOUNCE AND PRACTICE WRITING.

ز

END	MIDDLE	FIRST LETTER	STANDING ALONE
ـز	ـزـ	زـ	ز

SĪN

PRONOUNCE AND PRACTICE WRITING.

ﺮﺳ

END	MIDDLE	FIRST LETTER	STANDING ALONE
ﺲ	ﺴ	ﺳ	ﺱ

15

SHĪN

PRONOUNCE AND PRACTICE WRITING.

شر

END	MIDDLE	FIRST LETTER	STANDING ALONE
ش	ﺸ	ﺷ	ش

SAD

PRONOUNCE AND PRACTICE WRITING.

صٌ,

END	MIDDLE	FIRST LETTER	STANDING ALONE
ـص	ـصـ	صـ	ص

DAD

PRONOUNCE AND PRACTICE WRITING.

ﺿﺭ

END	MIDDLE	FIRST LETTER	STANDING ALONE
ﺾ	ﻀ	ﺿ	ض

18

TA

PRONOUNCE AND PRACTICE WRITING.

END	MIDDLE	FIRST LETTER	STANDING ALONE
ط	ط	ط	ط

ZAH

PRONOUNCE AND PRACTICE WRITING.

END	MIDDLE	FIRST LETTER	STANDING ALONE
ظ	ظ	ظ	ظ

20

'AIN

PRONOUNCE AND PRACTICE WRITING.

عٔ

END	MIDDLE	FIRST LETTER	STANDING ALONE
ح	ح	ع	ع

21

GHAIN

PRONOUNCE AND PRACTICE WRITING.

غ

END	MIDDLE	FIRST LETTER	STANDING ALONE
غ	غ	غ	غ

22

FEH

PRONOUNCE AND PRACTICE WRITING.

ف

END	MIDDLE	FIRST LETTER	STANDING ALONE
ـف	ـفـ	فـ	ف

QAF

PRONOUNCE AND PRACTICE WRITING.

ق

END	MIDDLE	FIRST LETTER	STANDING ALONE
ق	ﻘ	ﻗ	ق

KAF

PRONOUNCE AND PRACTICE WRITING.

كأ ↓
←

END	MIDDLE	FIRST LETTER	STANDING ALONE
كأ	ک	ک	كأ

LAM

PRONOUNCE AND PRACTICE WRITING.

ل

END	MIDDLE	FIRST LETTER	STANDING ALONE
ل	ل	ل	ل

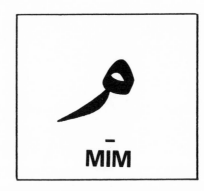

MĪM

PRONOUNCE AND PRACTICE WRITING.

END	MIDDLE	FIRST LETTER	STANDING ALONE

27

NŪN

PRONOUNCE AND PRACTICE WRITING.

ن

END	MIDDLE	FIRST LETTER	STANDING ALONE
ن	ـنـ	نـ	ن

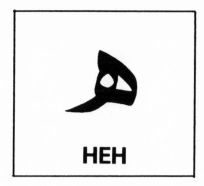

HEH

PRONOUNCE AND PRACTICE WRITING.

END	MIDDLE	FIRST LETTER	STANDING ALONE

29

WAW

PRONOUNCE AND PRACTICE WRITING.

و

END	MIDDLE	FIRST LETTER	STANDING ALONE
و	و	و	و

30

YEH

PRONOUNCE AND PRACTICE WRITING.

ي

END	MIDDLE	FIRST LETTER	STANDING ALONE
ي	ﻴ	ﻳ	ي

31

USING THE ALPHABET TO FORM WORDS. The following sets of words illustrate the use of each letter of the alphabet in a beginning, middle and end position. Arabic is written and read from right to left.

Arnab أرنب	farr فأر	yag'ra يقرأ

battat بطة	tabbila طبلة	kitaab كتاب

READ AND PRACTICE WRITING.

bint بنت	miftaah مفتاح	timsaah تمساح

mihraath محراث	Qeethara قيشارة	thalab ثعلب

33

READ AND PRACTICE WRITING.

دجاج dajaj	شجرة shajara	جمل Jamal

بلح balah	صحن sahn	حمامة hamama

READ AND PRACTICE WRITING.

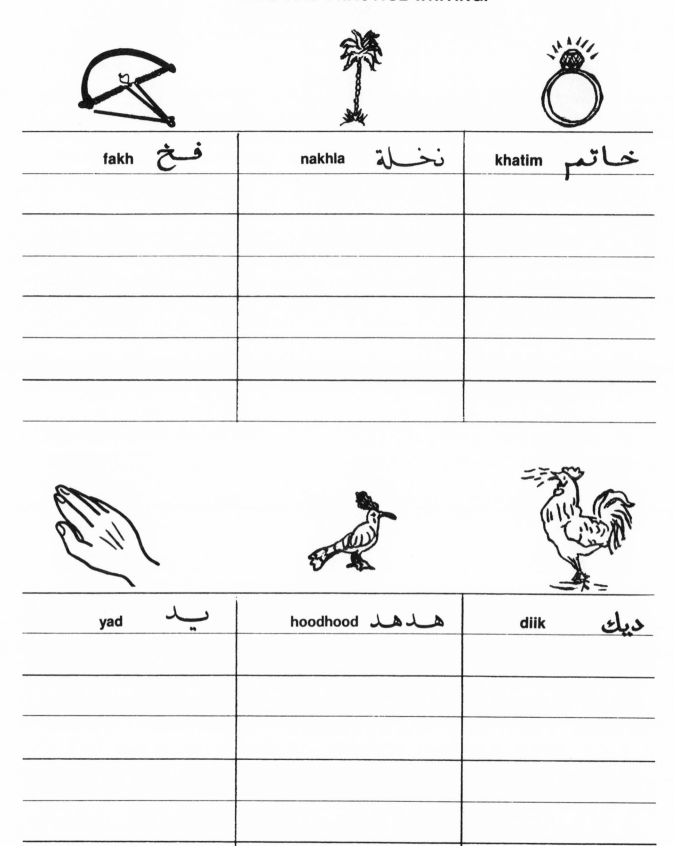

fakh فـخ	nakhla نخـلة	khatim خـاتـم

yad يـد	hoodhood هـدهـد	diik ديك

35

READ AND PRACTICE WRITING.

kunfoth قنفـذ	hitha حـذاء	thi'b ذئب

saqr صقر	markab مركب	rummana رمانة

READ AND PRACTICE WRITING.

زير zeer	وزة wazza	موز mawz

ساعة sa'a	مسطرة mastara	فاس faas

qirsh قرش	munshaar منشار	shamā شمعة

muqas مقص	asfour عصفور	suffara صفارة

READ AND PRACTICE WRITING.

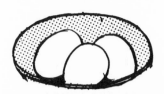  

bayd بيض	bayda بيضة	dab' ضبع

kutt قط	battikha بطيخة	tabla طبلة

READ AND PRACTICE WRITING.

mahafith محافظ	mahfathat محفظة	tharf ظرف

dafadi' ضفادع	na'ama نعامة	ayn عين

READ AND PRACTICE WRITING.

samgh صمغ	mighrafa مغرفة	guraab غراب

kharouf خروف	qafas قفص	feel فيل

READ AND PRACTICE WRITING.

qalam قلم	baqara بقرة	ta baq طبق

kalb كلب	sikkiina سكينة	samak سمك

42

READ AND PRACTICE WRITING.

gazaal غزال	sillum سلم	lahm لحم

qalam قلم	samaka سمكة	munshar منشار

43

READ AND PRACTICE WRITING.

nakhla نخلة	inab عنب	hissan حصان

haram هرم	fahed فهد	miyah مياه

READ AND PRACTICE WRITING.

warda وردة	mawz موز	dalu دلو

yammaama يمامة	tayyaara طيارة	gidi جدي

PUT SCRAMBLED LETTERS INTO WORDS

أ ـ ق ـ ر

_____

ر ـ ش ـ ب

_____

ز ـ ع ـ ر

_____

ب ـ ل ـ ع

_____

ض ـ ب ـ ي

_____

ن ـ ي ـ ع

_____

INSERT MISSING LETTER

أرن...

...لب

...زة

ور...ة

جَ...ل

...بلة

46

FILL IN THE CORRECT WORDS

PRACTICE WRITING NUMBERS ONE TO TEN

SITTA	WAHHAD
٦	١
SAB'A	ITHNAN
٧	٢
THAMANIYA	THALATHA
٨	٣
TESS'A	ARBA'A
٩	٤
ASHARA	KHAMSA
١٠	٥

READ THESE WORDS.

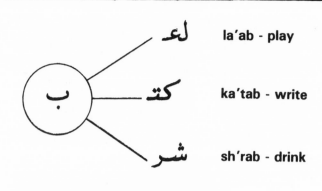

 لعـ la'ab - play

كتـ ka'tab - write

شـر sh'rab - drink

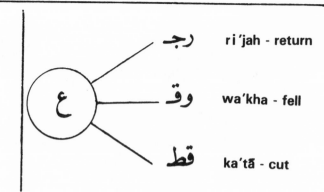

رجـ ri'jah - return

وقـ wa'kha - fell

قط ka'tā - cut

READ THESE SENTENCES.

رجع الديك إلى شجرة .

عمر يلعب مع القطة .

عمر يقرأ في الكتاب

عادل يشرب ماء .

أحمد وقع من سلم .

عادل قطف وردة .

48

(١)	السَّبْتُ	'as-sabt	Saturday
(٢)	الأَحَدُ	'al'ahad	Sunday
(٣)	الإثنـين	'al'ithnayn	Monday
(٤)	الثُّلاثاءُ	'ath-thulaathaa'	Tuesday
(٥)	الأَربِـعاءُ	'al'arbi'aa'	Wednesday
(٦)	الخَميسُ	'alkhamees	Thursday
(٧)	الجُمُعَةُ	'al jumu'a	Friday

أَيَّامُ الأُسْبُوعِ   (أ)

The days of the week

(ب) مُلاحَظَة: الجُمُعةُ يَومُ آلعُطْلَةِ آلأُسْبوعِيَّةِ

Friday is the weekend

تَدْريبات   Exercises

أُكْتُبْ أَيّامَ الأُسْبوعِ بآللغةِ آلعَرَبِيّةِ ؟

Write the days of the week in Arabic?

(١) ....

(٢) ....

(٣) ....

(٤) ....

(٥) ....

(٦) ....

(٧) ....

49

OTHER ARABIC LANGUAGE PUBLICATIONS

Learn Arabic Thru Words and Simple Phrases
by Lily Sayegh.
This book follows the *First Arabic Handwriting Workbook*, and is designed to teach students to read, pronounce and practice writing Arabic words and phrases. $7.95

Arabic Vocabulary Cards
1000 1x3 Cards
A quick and enjoyable way to build basic vocabulary in Arabic. This set is comprised of more than 1000 standard Arabic vocabulary words. Knowledge of Arabic required. $10.95

Teach Yourself Arabic by J. R. Smart
The Arabic taught in this book is the written and spoken language of the Arab World. This book is a clearly structured introductory course designed to help you achieve fluency in modern Arabic.
Book and Two Audio Cassettes $24.95

Arabic Verbs and Essentials of Grammar by Jane Wightwick.
Ideal for students of all levels, this practical language guide provides an accessible introduction to Arabic grammar and comprehensive explanation of verbs.
128 pages. $12.95

First Lessons in Literary Arabic by McCarus.
This book is designed to teach beginning students to read modern Arabic. It is also designed to teach students to read modern literary Arabic with acceptable pronunciation and the ability to write.$12.95

Learn to Read Arabic by Raja Nasr
A good elementary to intermediate Arabic reader. Twenty-three lessons present a concise explanation of the writing system. Original Arabic stories written in Arabic script with the English translation.
Book and Cassette $14.95

Arabs: Activities for Elementary School
Activities, games, cultural information, nursery rhymes, folktales, cooking, and dancing are just some of the things in this activity book. A wonderful teaching aid for the classroom. In English. 62 pages. Paperbound. 1991. $18.95

Arab World Mosaic by Rodseth, Howell, Shryock
A curriculum supplement for elementary teachers. This much needed resource includes units on the family, home , holidays, folktales, cultural note, and more. Paperbound. 208 pages. $20.00

Wortabet English-Arabic; Arabic-English Dictionary by Wortabet and Porter
An English to Arabic, and Arabic to English edition of this popular dictionary. Contains Arabic script with English translations, and a supplement of new words. 900 pages.
Hardbound $24.95
Paperbound $18.95

Arabic Proverbs by Joseph Hankit
This bilingual collection of proverbs contains over 600 Arabic proverbs written in colloquial Arabic with side by side English translations, and where appropriate, explanation of the custom which gave rise to the proverbs. Attractive, fascinating and very enjoyable. 144 pages. $11.95

International Book Centre, Inc.
2391 Auburn Road
Shelby Twp., Michigan 48317
Telephone: (248) 879-8436

Visit our Website at www.ibcbooks.com
E-mail # ibc@ibcbooks